Generation STEM

What Girls Say about Science, Technology, Engineering, and Math

This report was made possible in part by a generous contribution from Lockheed Martin.

girl scouts

National President
Connie L. Lindsey

Chief Executive Officer
Anna Maria Chávez

Chief of External Affairs
Timothy Higdon

Vice President, Research, Girl Scout Research Institute
Michael Conn, Ph.D.

Authors, Girl Scout Research Institute
Kamla Modi, Ph.D., Research and Outreach Analyst
Judy Schoenberg, Ed. M., Director, Research and Outreach
Kimberlee Salmond, M.P.P., Senior Researcher, Research and Outreach

Conducted in conjunction with Teenage Research Unlimited

Acknowledgment is made to the following individuals who provided expert feedback on the report: Christianne Corbett, Senior Researcher, American Association of University Women (AAUW); Catherine Didion, Senior Program Officer, National Academy of Engineering (NAE); Randy Freedman, M.Ed., Outreach Manager, Society of Women Engineers (SWE); Preeti Gupta, Ph.D., Senior Vice President for Education and Family Programs, New York Hall of Science; Thea Sahr, Director of Programs, National Engineers Week Foundation; and Andresse St. Rose, Ed.D., Senior Researcher, AAUW.

We would like to thank the following individuals at GSUSA for their contributions to this research study: Wendy Friedman, Ph.D., Project Manager, GSRI; Alice Hockenbury, Director of Advocacy, Public Policy, and Advocacy; and Claudia Rincón, Ph.D., Senior Researcher, GSRI. Acknowledgement is made to Lynn Obee for editing and Julita Ehle and Chris Brody for design.

Acknowledgment is also made to the following individuals from the Girl Scout councils for their contributions: Lani Connolly, Ph.D., GSLE Director, Girl Scouts of Northeast Texas; Emily Fletcher, Director of Programs, Girl Scouts of Northeast Ohio; Amy Hee Kim, Ph.D., Manager, STEM program, Girl Scouts of Greater Los Angeles; Tiffany Lemons, Director of Research, Development, and Evaluation, Girl Scouts of Central Indiana; and Carlyn Nelson, STEM Specialist, Girl Scouts of Chesapeake Bay.

We would like to thank the staff and members of Girl Scouts of Central Indiana and Girl Scouts of Chesapeake Bay for their participation.

The Girl Scout Research Institute expresses special appreciation to the girls who participated in this study.

© 2012 by Girl Scouts of the USA

All rights reserved.

First Impression 2012
ISBN: 978-0-88441-793-4
10 9 8 7 6 5 4 3 2 1

Contents

INTRODUCTION 2
Background and Research Goals
Why STEM, Why Now?
What We Know: The Context
The Current Study

THE FINDINGS 8
1. Girls Like STEM!
2. The Creative and Problem Solving Aspects of STEM Draw Girls
3. The DNA of a "STEM Girl" Sets Her Apart
4. A Gap Exists between STEM Interest and Career Choice
5. The Story Differs for African American and Hispanic Girls

SUMMARY AND DISCUSSION 25
Implications and Recommendations for Future Work

APPENDIX 31
Methodology

REFERENCES 32

RESOURCES 34

Introduction

Over the past 50 years, women in the United States have made great strides in education and entry into the work force in this country. However, despite these advances, women continue to be underrepresented in the fields of science, technology, engineering, and math, collectively referred to as "STEM." Women's representation is low at all levels of the STEM career "pipeline," from interest and intent to majoring in a STEM field in college to having a career in a STEM field in adulthood. Studies show that girls lose interest in math and science during middle school, and STEM interest for girls is low, compared to boys. Most research on this topic has focused on representation of girls and women in these fields, primarily on the obstacles preventing more girls and women from entering them. It is time now to shift the focus toward understanding and developing solutions for "what works" for girls who show interest and engage in the fields of STEM.

The goal of the Girl Scout Research Institute (GSRI) is to elevate the voices of girls on issues that matter to them and their futures. The aim of this report is to explore how girls can better become engaged in STEM through examination of what girls themselves say are their interests and perceptions about these important fields. We found encouraging results that we think offer new insights into how to keep girls engaged in STEM fields over time. Our findings both dispel myths about girls and STEM, and give a deeper understanding about girls who are actively interested in STEM and are seemingly on the path to STEM careers. These findings, we believe, will lead to more comprehensive solutions to the underrepresentation of women in the STEM workforce. We found that:

- Seventy-four percent of high school girls across the country are interested in the fields and subjects of STEM.
- Girls are interested in the process of learning, asking questions, and problem solving.
- Girls want to help people and make a difference in the world.
- Girls who are interested in STEM are high achievers who have supportive adult networks and are exposed to STEM fields.
- Girls who are interested in STEM fields are actually interested in many subjects and career opportunities—STEM is just one area of interest among many.
- Perceived gender barriers are still high for girls and may help explain why STEM fields aren't their top career choices.
- African American and Hispanic girls have high interest in STEM, high confidence, and a strong work ethic, but have fewer supports, less exposure, and lower academic achievement than Caucasian girls.

This research can help to change the discussion on girls and STEM by offering a much needed strength-based perspective focusing on what contexts are most supportive for girls. We hope this research helps to take the conversation to the next level by focusing on how to use girls' interests to cultivate career plans for them in STEM fields.

Background and Research Goals

A study on girls and STEM is timely and important for a number of reasons. Research points to continued underrepresentation of women in STEM careers, despite their high achievement in academics and other career fields. STEM education has become a top priority of the United States government and national organizations, which recognize the need to expand opportunities for STEM involvement and to fill STEM jobs in this country.

In order to contribute to this dialogue and to determine how Girl Scouts could offer effective solutions, the GSRI conducted a large scale study consisting of a literature review and qualitative and quantitative methodologies designed to better understand how interest in STEM can be developed in girls. (See appendix for full methodology.) Specifically, we were interested in investigating:

- How girls perceive STEM subjects and fields
- What factors encourage or discourage girls' interest and engagement in STEM (such as the role of adults' support, exposure to STEM careers, personal characteristics, stereotypes)
- What girls' future career plans are, and if they include STEM

Why STEM? Why Now?

Expertise in STEM fields promotes inventiveness, scientific discovery, and efficiency in the way things are done, while also opening up new job and economic opportunities. Due to technological advances, STEM jobs in the United States in the past ten years have grown at three times the pace of non-STEM jobs, and are projected to continue growing at this pace through the next decade.[i] STEM jobs require technical expertise, specialized training, or higher education, making the typical job seeker in the United States underqualified for a job in a STEM field. As a result, there are not enough qualified job candidates in the United States to fill all of these projected positions, even during this time of high unemployment.

The United States ranks lower than several Asian and European nations in math and science achievement. Eighth graders in the United States are ranked tenth globally in both math and science achievement, behind a number of Asian countries, including Japan, Korea, China, Singapore, and Hong Kong SAR.[ii] Likewise, research shows that high achievers in math in the United States are most likely to be Asian American or foreign born,[iii] which mirrors the high percentage of people who fill American jobs in technology, computing, engineering, and math. Research points to cultural and social stigmas about math achievement in the United States that prevent both United States-born Caucasian and underrepresented minority girls and boys from achieving their full potential in this subject area.[iii] STEM education and enrichment are currently national priorities set by the United States government through initiatives such as Change the Equation and Educate to Innovate. It is a top priority for researchers, policymakers, educators, and youth developmental experts who agree that investing in our youth to succeed in math and science will produce positive results for our country's future.

Over the past 20 years, researchers and practitioners have intensified their efforts to promote gender equity in STEM education through research-based advances in educational programming in schools, homes, and other enrichment settings. A wide range of programs and initiatives are in place,[iv, v] including within Girl Scouts of the USA. Girl Scouts reach 2.4 million girls ages 5-17, making this organization uniquely positioned to address gender equity in STEM education and enrichment across the country. Through program partnerships with various organizations, such as Lockheed Martin, Motorola, the National Science Foundation, NASA, *FIRST*, and AT&T, Girl Scouts has been committed to providing STEM programming to girls through activities aimed at engaging and cultivating interest in STEM fields. In addition, Girl Scouts of the USA and its councils across the country have embarked on an advocacy initiative to raise awareness about girls' participation in STEM with public officials and community leaders at the local, state, and federal levels. The organization is fulfilling the Girl Scout mission to be the voice for girls by sharing its knowledge and expertise with the larger community to ensure that all girls have what they need to succeed in STEM fields.

Nonetheless, research shows that there are several cultural, social, and individual factors preventing more girls and women from entering and having careers in STEM fields.

What We Know: The Context

Women and Girls in STEM

Women are faring better, academically, than ever before. Today, the majority of college graduates (57%) and master's level graduates (60%) are women,[vi] and nearly half (48%) of this country's work force is comprised of women.[vii]

However, there are some fields in which female representation has remained low. Within STEM fields women are better represented in life sciences, chemistry, and mathematics; women are not well represented in engineering, computing, and physics.

- Women account for about only 20% of the bachelor's degrees in engineering, computer science, and physics[viii, ix]
- Regardless of specific area of STEM, only about 25% of these positions are held by women.[x]

Researchers and experts in STEM education agree that boosting the number of women in STEM fields would expand our nation's pool of workers, educators, and innovators for the future, bring a new dimension to the work, and potentially tackle problems that have been overlooked in the past.

Achievement in Math and Science

Although there is an age-old belief that girls are not high achievers in math and science, but rather, are stronger in English/language arts and social studies, performance measures paint a different picture. According to the American Association of University Women, high school girls and boys perform equally well in math and science. Specifically, high school girls earn more math and science credits than do boys; and girls' GPAs, aggregated across math and science classes, are higher than boys. Boys, however, tend to do better on standardized tests, such as the SAT or ACT.[xi]

However, a number of factors are known to reduce performance, and likely have influenced perceptions of girls' ability to achieve in math and science:

- *Outdated stereotypes and feelings of insufficiency can hold girls back.* Social psychological research shows that the stereotype that girls are not as good as boys in math can have negative consequences. When girls know or are made aware of this stereotype, they perform much more poorly than boys; however, when they are told that boys and girls perform equally well on a test, there is no gender difference.[xii, xiii] It is possible that girls are internalizing this stereotype and talking themselves out of achieving in math and science when, in reality, they are doing just as well or better than boys. This stereotype threat has also been found for African American and Hispanic students in test achievement.[xiv]

- *The subtleties of society and culture reflect the stereotype that girls are not good at or suited for math and science and unconsciously discourage girls.* For example, experts in STEM education have observed how mothers interact with their children in science museum settings, finding that mothers encourage their sons more than their daughters to engage in hands-on activities in museums.[xv]

- *Compared to boys, girls with the same abilities are more likely to give up when the material is difficult and to talk themselves out of pursuing the field.*[xvi, xvii] Research has also shown that having confidence in one's ability and believing that hard work and effort can increase intelligence are associated with higher achievement in math and science among girls.[xvi] This and other research suggest that perception of one's ability or capability is more important for a girl than her actual ability or knowledge, and changing this perception can lead to more entry into STEM domains.

Interest in Math and Science

Research shows that girls start losing interest in math and science during middle school.[xviii] Girls are typically more interested in careers where they can help others (e.g., teaching, child care, working with animals)[xix] and make the world a better place.[xx] Recent surveys have shown that girls and young women are much less interested than boys and young men in math and science. A national report on college freshmen major/career interests shows that on average, 20% of young women intend to major in a STEM field, compared to 50% of young men.[xxi] Four consecutive years of data show that these numbers increase for young men over time (from 45% to 56%), but do not increase for young women. Another recent poll showed that 32% of girls ages 13-17 thought that computing would be a good college major, compared to 74% of boys in the same age range.[xxii] This lack of interest may be a product of older stereotypes about girls doing poorly in math, or of low confidence in their abilities, or alternatively may reflect a general well-roundedness in girls that leads many to turn to their high verbal skills during career planning.[xxiii]

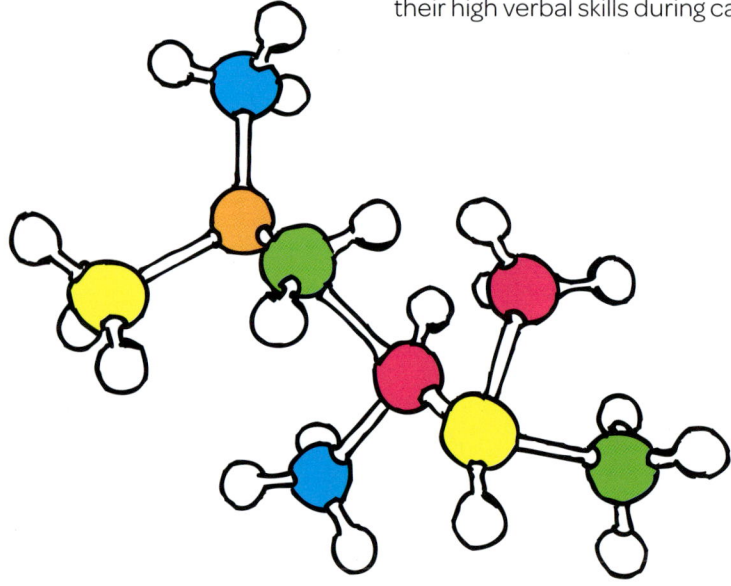

Pursuing a STEM Career

The workplace environment for women in STEM appears to be somewhat inhospitable to the needs of women. A study of female engineering college graduates across the United States shows that among an already low 20% of female engineering graduates, only 11% are practicing engineering in this country.[xxiv] When asked why so many dropped out of engineering fields, participants' reasons were due to the intensity of the workplace environment (including long hours, heavy travel time), lack of opportunities to advance in their careers, and low salary. Additionally, a recent report from the U.S. Department of Commerce found that only 26% of women with a STEM college degree have entered a STEM career.[i] The remaining women who drop out end up going into other careers, such as business or education.

To summarize, the research shows that although girls perform as well in math and science as boys, there continue to be biases and factors relating to a perception of lower achievement for girls. Additionally, retention in STEM careers is low for women.

The Current Study

Past research has focused heavily on barriers and reasons why there aren't more girls or women in STEM. This report heads in a different direction: It puts a spotlight on girls' perceptions, attitudes, and abilities to pursue STEM fields now and in the future by using a strength-based perspective in order to identify and explore contexts in which girls may thrive in STEM subjects. In addition, the study sought to understand girls' perspectives and levels of interest in STEM fields in order to expand opportunities for girls at large.

A mixed-method qualitative and quantitative design was employed for this study. The qualitative portion consisted of focus groups with girls in several regions across the country and the quantitative portion consisted of a national sample group of 852 teen girls. The study looked at girls who were interested in STEM subjects and fields as well as girls who were not interested in these fields in order to understand how they differed in terms of support, exposure, aspirations, and the like. (For more details on methodology, please see appendix.)

The next section focuses on the five main findings of the quantitative survey. All results reported were statistically significant (at 95% confidence level) unless otherwise stated. Where appropriate, girls' quotes from focus groups are interwoven with these top findings for further illustration and recommendations for future work. Also included is feedback from experts in STEM fields demonstrating their reactions to the research findings as well as recommendations for future research, programming, and policy efforts.

Finding 1: Girls Like STEM!

Girls are overwhelmingly interested in STEM. Our findings show that a total of 74% of teen girls are interested in STEM. Interest in STEM was defined as responding "somewhat" or "very" interested in the general field of STEM and in a STEM subject, such as science, math, engineering, or computer science/information technology.

After determining overall incidence of girls' interest in STEM (74%), groups of interest and non-interest were equalized for statistical comparisons. The following results (2-5) demonstrate these group differences. "STEM girls" refer to girls who are interested in STEM, and "non-STEM girls" refer to girls who are not interested in STEM.

Finding 2: The Creative and Problem Solving Aspects of STEM Draw Girls

Girls interested in STEM like to understand how things work (87% vs. 65% non-STEM girls), solve problems (85% vs. 70% non-STEM girls), do hands-on activities (83% vs. 56% non-STEM girls), and ask questions (80% vs. 54% non-STEM girls).

% WHO AGREE…	STEM	NON-STEM
I like to understand how things work.	**87**	65
I like puzzles and solving problems.	**85**	70
I like doing hands-on science projects.	**83**	56
I like asking questions about how things work and finding ways to answer them.	**80**	54
I like to understand how the natural world works.	**79**	57
I like building things or putting things together.	**67**	47
I like to understand how things are built.	**66**	47
I like doing math problems.	**65**	32
I think it would be fun to create an iPhone app or design a computer/video game.*	**62**	57

*significant only at 90% confidence level

Focus group data showed similar interests in facets of STEM, including the process, the excitement of solving puzzles and problems, and the idea that STEM could allow girls to do something new and innovative in a career:

> *I love science and I like seeing how things work. I think I did a lot of engineering on my own when I was little. I love to take things apart and see if I can get them back together. I always try to figure out how things work.*
>
> —preteen girl, Austin, Texas

> *I think [STEM jobs] can be very rewarding in the end when you get the result that you were looking for, or when you find a completely different result than what you were looking for; just knowing that you were able to start from a question or hypothesis and work to find this result that could possibly make a big difference in people's lives.*
>
> —teen girl, Indianapolis, Indiana

The degree to which STEM fields can tap into girls' inquisitive thought processes may indicate ways in which more girls can become attracted to these fields.

Hands-on activities are reflected as important for STEM education in focus groups as well:

> *When I was in lower grades, it was pretty fun to do activities in science. When I got to sixth grade, we just had to do book work and questions. Science wasn't my favorite anymore.*
>
> —preteen girl, Wilmington, Delaware

Finding 3: The DNA of a "STEM Girl" Sets Her Apart

Compared to girls who aren't interested in STEM fields, girls interested in STEM fields ("STEM girls") are higher achievers, better students, have stronger support systems, and have been exposed to STEM fields.

Interest and Achievement in STEM Subjects

We wanted to identify the characteristics of girls who are interested in STEM fields, such as the qualities that set them apart, their personal attributes, and the supports they have in place.

Girls interested in STEM are better students and more academically engaged overall than non-STEM girls. STEM girls have higher interest in most academic subjects, including non-STEM subjects such as social studies and foreign languages. STEM girls have higher self-reported grades in STEM subjects than non-STEM girls, as well as higher self-reported overall grades (3.65 for STEM girls vs. 3.52 for non-STEM girls).

Confidence

Compared to non-STEM girls, STEM girls have higher confidence in their academic abilities.

- Girls interested in STEM fields believe that they are smart enough to have a career in STEM (92% vs. 68% non-STEM girls).
- Three-quarters (71%) of STEM girls claim they are smarter than other girls their age, compared to half (51%) of non-STEM girls.

% WHO AGREE…	STEM	NON-STEM
I'm smart enough to have a career in STEM.	92	68
I am smarter than other girls my age.	71	51
I am more driven than other girls my age.	64	48

Goals and Aspirations

STEM girls have higher academic goals and aspirations for themselves.

- They say they are very likely to get a good education (e.g., 92% of STEM girls expect to go to graduate school, compared to 75% of non-STEM girls).
- They are less likely to say that they will become famous one day (29% vs. 40% non-STEM), likely attributing their future success to their internal abilities rather than external forces (e.g., being noticed).

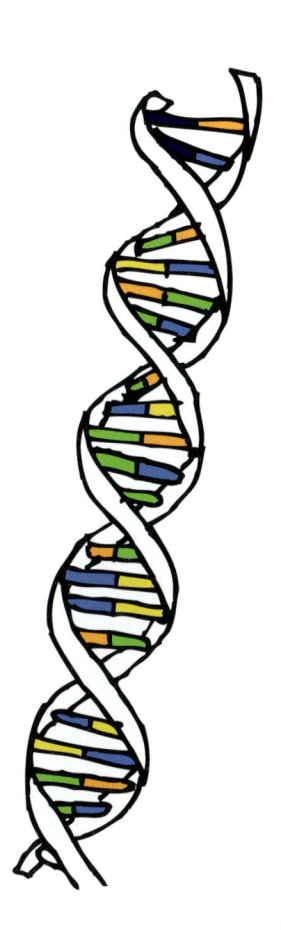

% LIKELIHOOD THAT THEY WILL…	STEM	NON-STEM
Graduate from college	98	95
Go to graduate school	92	75
Make a lot of money	93	89
Make as much or more money than their significant other	85	79
Become famous	29	41

Hard Work and Persistence

STEM girls seem to be more inclined to grapple with adversity and overcome obstacles than non-STEM girls. STEM girls consider themselves hard workers (93% vs. 87% non-STEM) and feel that "obstacles make me stronger" (91% vs. 85% of non-STEM girls). STEM girls overwhelmingly feel that "Whatever boys can do, girls can do" (97% vs. 91% of non-STEM girls). It should be noted that all girls we surveyed scored high on these factors. Girls in general appear to be highly driven, seek out challenges, and set higher goals for themselves.

% WHO AGREE…	STEM	NON-STEM
Whatever boys can do, girls can do.	97	91
If I try really hard at something, I know I will succeed.	95	88
I'm a hard worker.	93	87
When someone tells me I can't do something, I try to prove them wrong.	94	89
Obstacles make me stronger.	91	85
I get frustrated if something is too hard.	79	86
I try to pursue things I'm naturally good at and avoid things that are hard for me.	66	79

Girls engaged in focus group discussions mirrored these points:

> *I know that girls have accomplished a lot and handle a lot more stress than boys. People count on them to do everything and so girls work harder than boys most of the time. [We] have more to prove, that yes, we can do it better.*
> —preteen girl, Orlando, Florida

These characteristics are particularly useful for STEM fields:

> *I think [obstacles] would help me thrive in my job. I'm okay with doing a lot of hard work as long as I'm getting a job done and I'm doing it right. The minimal margin for error—I think that would help me try and stay on my toes all the time, be prepared for anything, and make sure I knew that I was doing it properly, so I think that would help me be the best at my job.*
> —teen girl, Indianapolis, Indiana

Exposure to STEM Fields

Girls who are interested in STEM have had greater exposure to STEM fields than girls who are not interested in STEM. Two-thirds (66% vs. 47% non-STEM) know someone in a STEM career, and half (53% vs. 36% non-STEM) know a woman in a STEM career. A majority of girls who are not interested in STEM (79% vs. 60% of STEM girls) know more about other careers than they do about STEM. This is an important component further explained through focus groups:

> *If you think about teachers, everyone knows about teachers as a career, but not everyone our age really thinks about engineering. They don't know all that much about it.*
> —preteen girl, Wilmington, Delaware

Exposure was also higher in terms of experience in STEM activities. STEM girls were more likely to have done hands-on science activities when they were younger (51% vs. 37% of non-STEM girls), gone to science/tech museums (66% vs. 55% non-STEM), and engaged in an extracurricular STEM activity (36% vs. 13% non-STEM).

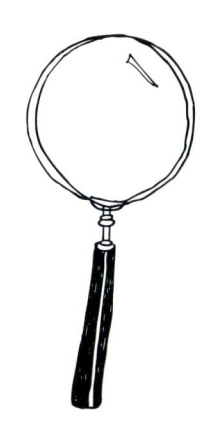

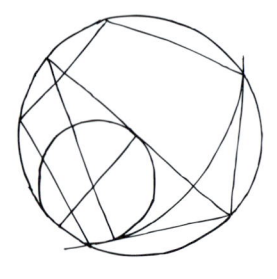

% WHO AGREE...	STEM	NON-STEM
My parents try hard to make sure I'm exposed to many career options.	70	63
I know more about other careers than I do about careers in STEM.	60	79
I know a lot about my career options in STEM.	54	31
I know someone in a STEM career.	66	47
I know a woman in a STEM career.	53	36
I have gone to science or technology museums.	66	55
I did hands-on science activities at home when I was younger.	51	37
I have participated in STEM activities outside of school such as camps, after-school programs, etc.	36	13

Adult Supports

STEM girls have stronger support networks overall in the planning of their careers and futures. STEM girls have more career support from parents, family members, family friends, teachers, and friends, compared to non-STEM girls. In particular, parents play a key role through their interest and support of girls' pursuing STEM. For example, 76% of STEM girls say their parents have pushed them to think about what they want to do when they grow up, compared to 67% of non-STEM girls.

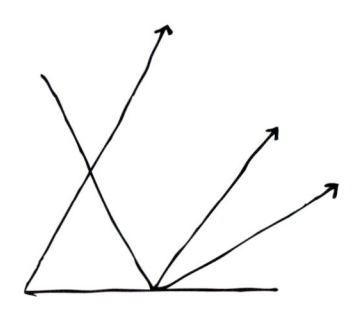

% WOULD SUPPORT THEIR PURSUING A STEM CAREER...	STEM	NON-STEM
Mom	96	86
Dad	95	88
Other family members	84	77
Teachers*	82	77
Friends	79	71
Siblings	73	64
Other adult friends/mentors**	68	63

*significant only at 90% confidence level
**not statistically significant

% AGREEMENT FOR DAD/MOM	STEM	NON-STEM
He/she thinks I am smart enough to have any career I want.	**92**	85
He/she pushes me to think about what I want to be when I grow up.	**76**	66

Two-thirds (65%) of mothers of STEM girls encourage their girls to pursue STEM, compared to one-third (32%) of non-STEM girls. Fathers also play a key role in STEM encouragement:

- Nearly three-quarters (71%) of STEM girls report that their fathers are very interested in STEM, compared to 52% of non-STEM girls.
- More than two-thirds (68%) of STEM girls report that their fathers encourage them to pursue STEM, compared to 35% of non-STEM girls.

% WHO AGREE…	STEM	NON-STEM
My dad is very interested in STEM.	**71**	52
My mom is very interested in STEM.	**45**	32
My dad encourages me to pursue STEM.	**68**	35
My mom encourages me to pursue STEM.	**65**	32

Focus group discussions showed us the unique role that fathers have in encouraging their daughters to pursue STEM. Although mothers' encouragement is important, fathers are more likely to be working in STEM fields and can model success and a sense of connection for girls who may not naturally consider these fields.

> *My dad is a chemist, he inspired me.*
> —teen girl, Seattle, Washington

> *My dad always tells me this is where you have the potential… not arts, but engineering. Having parents that push you or let you think about it. Support you with whatever you do. If you have the support it makes you believe in it, even if nobody else does.*
> —teen girl, Austin, Texas

Finding 4: A Gap Exists Between STEM Interest and Career Choice

Interest in STEM fields doesn't necessarily translate into choosing one of these fields for a career. Although interest in STEM is high, few girls consider it their number one career choice, given competing opportunities and interests.

A high 81% of STEM girls express interest in pursuing a career in a STEM field—specifically, in engineering, physical/life science, math, computer science/information technology, or software development. However, only 13% say that it is their first choice.*

Two-thirds of STEM girls are interested in medicine/healthcare (careers such as a doctor, veterinarian, nurse, pharmacist, dentist) as a career choice and STEM girls choose this field as their number one choice over any other career (30%).

Other Interests of STEM Girls

STEM girls are interested in a wide variety of STEM and non-STEM subjects. The top four ranked careers of interest are medicine/healthcare (65%), arts/design (64%), social science (60%), and entertainment (59%). STEM careers are not as highly ranked, when compared to other career categories.

Additionally, one-third of girls (30% STEM, 34% non-STEM) are interested in being stay-at-home moms.

*****STEM girls who say that STEM is a top career priority (13%) are passionate and committed to STEM. They are more likely to say they are 'very interested' in STEM subjects and fields, they are more interested in hands-on activities, and they are more likely to describe STEM subjects as fun, exciting, and subjects their parents think they should pursue.

% INTERESTED IN PURSUING...	STEM	NON-STEM
Medicine/Healthcare	65	32
Arts/Design	64	70
Social Science	60	48
Entertainment	59	67
Communications/Media**	58	59
Physical/Life Sciences	57	15
Community/Social Services**	57	51
Education*	44	38
Business/Finance	43	29
Law	41	30
Engineering	32	3
Math	31	5
Architecture	30	16
Stay-at-home mom**	30	34
Computer Science/Information Technology	27	11
Software Development	25	13
Protective Services	22	15
Manufacturing/Production**	15	13
Armed Forces	14	8
Construction/Installation/Maintenance/Repair	8	3

*significant only at 90% confidence
**not statistically significant

> We find that many girls and educators don't know what engineering is or the reality of making this a career choice. I find it especially interesting that almost no girls (3%) who identify as not interested in STEM would choose engineering. It shows me that beyond other challenges, engineering has an image problem that needs to be changed.
>
> Randy Freedman, M.Ed.
> Outreach Manager, Society of Women Engineers (SWE)

Career Motivations

Nearly all girls (98%) wish to be in a career that they love. More STEM girls have philanthropic motivations such as helping people (94% vs. 83% non-STEM) and making a difference in the world (92% vs. 82%), compared to non-STEM girls. Additionally, STEM girls are motivated by being in a career that requires them to think (87% STEM vs. 75% non-STEM) and a career that changes the way people do things (77% STEM vs. 66% non-STEM). Interestingly, although STEM girls are motivated by philanthropic desires, choosing a STEM career which can realize those desires still isn't coming out on top.

% IMPORTANCE IN CHOOSING A CAREER PATH	STEM	NON-STEM
Helping people	94	83
Making a difference in the world	92	82
Helping those who are less fortunate	88	80
Having input into how the job is done	88	82
Making a lot of money	87	81
Being in a career that requires you to think	87	75
Practicing a subject that you love most at school	87	75
Collaborating/working with others	81	74
Being in a career that changes the way people do things	77	66
Being in a career that requires creativity	76	82
Helping the environment	73	65
Being able to work with your hands	71	61
Being in a career that your parents approve of	63	52
Being in charge of others	47	37

What Holds Girls Back: Gender Barriers

Regardless of STEM interest, there continue to be barriers associated with STEM interest and involvement.

- More than half (57%) of all girls say that girls their age don't typically consider a career in STEM.
- Nearly half (47%) of all girls say that they would feel uncomfortable being the only girl in a group or class.
- Further, 57% of all girls say that if they went into a STEM career, they'd have to work harder than a man just to be taken seriously.

> *I think some girls don't want to do [STEM] because they don't think it's something girls should do. It's a boy subject; they should stay far away from it.*
> —teen girl, Indianapolis, Indiana

It is quite possible that these negative associations create barriers that keep girls from making STEM careers their top choices. As long as these stereotypes and barriers persist, they will likely impact whether girls ultimately consider STEM fields as viable options for their futures. Girls will continue to feed into these barriers or choose to fight them.

It is amazing that so many girls are interested in STEM. Our work must now turn to transforming this interest into action. It is particularly troubling that even among STEM-interested girls only 32% aspire to engineering. Engineering is a field that allows girls to actualize their dreams of making a difference, collaborating, and helping people, all while making a great salary.

Thea Sahr, M.Ed., Director of Programs, National Engineers Week Foundation

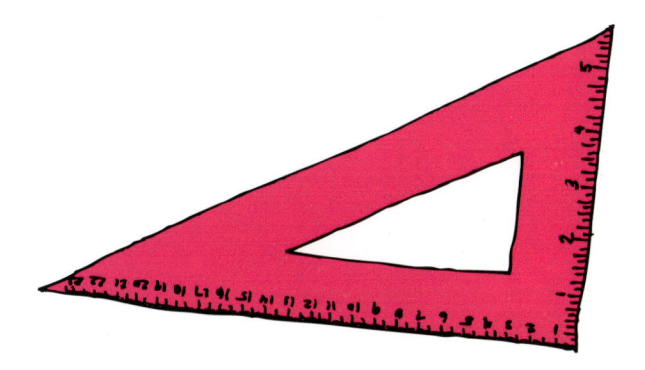

Finding 5: The Story Differs for African American and Hispanic Girls

We found some significant racial/ethnic group differences in our data. Specifically, we found that African American and Hispanic girls say they have just as much interest in STEM as Caucasian girls, but they have had less exposure to STEM, less adult support for pursuing STEM fields, lower academic achievement, and greater awareness of gender barriers in STEM professions. However, their confidence and ability to overcome obstacles are high, pointing to the strong role of individual characteristics in STEM interest and perceived ability in these subjects.

High Interest

Although interest in STEM is high for all ethnic groups (73% of Caucasian girls, 76% of African American girls, 74% of Hispanic girls), interest in some aspects of STEM is higher for African American and Hispanic girls. African American and Hispanic girls are more interested in:

- How things work (African American—82%, Hispanic—83%, Caucasian—73%)
- Building things/putting things together (African American—58%, Hispanic—67%, Caucasian—56%)
- Creating an iPhone app or designing a computer or video game (African American—67%, Hispanic—68%, Caucasian—55%).

% WHO AGREE…	CAUCASIAN	AFRICAN AMERICAN	HISPANIC
I like to understand how things work.[1]	75	**82**	**83**
I think it would be fun to create an iPhone app or design a computer/video game.[1]	55	**67**	**68**
I like building things or putting things together.[2]	56	58	**67**
I like to understand how things are built.**	57	57	64
I like puzzles and solving problems.**	77	81	80
I like doing hands-on science projects.**	70	74	73

[1] African American, Hispanic higher than Caucasian
[2] Hispanic significantly higher than Caucasian
**no statistical significance in these ethnic differences

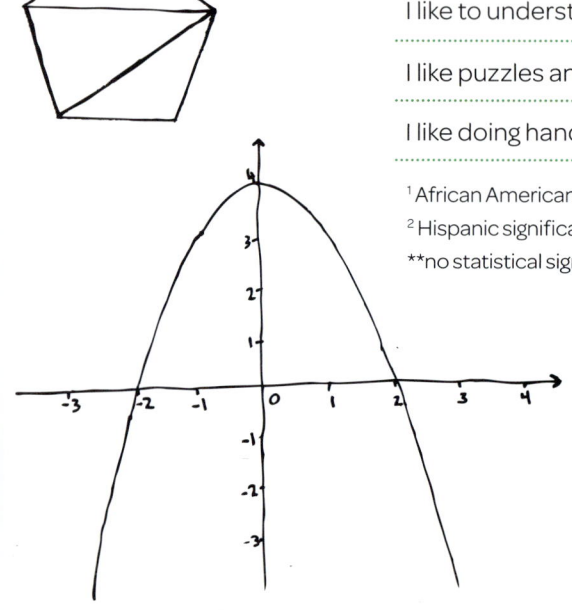

Confidence and Hard Work

African American and Hispanic girls are confident in their abilities and consider themselves hard workers. Nearly all girls (regardless of racial/ethnic background) consider themselves hard workers, believe "whatever boys can do, girls can do," (African American—97%, Hispanic—94%, Caucasian—94%) and "if I try really hard at something, I know I will succeed" (African American—93%, Hispanic—92%, Caucasian—92%).

Achievement, Exposure, Support

However, compared to Caucasian girls, African American and Hispanic girls score lower in some areas, including academic achievement, exposure to STEM careers, and adult support of STEM careers. African American and Hispanic girls both have lower self-reported grades in school than Caucasian girls (African American GPA—3.3; Hispanic GPA—3.4; Caucasian GPA—3.6).

In addition to academic achievement, STEM exposure is also lower for African American and Hispanic girls:

- Caucasian girls (61%) are more likely to know someone in a STEM career, compared to African American (48%) and Hispanic (52%) girls.
- Caucasian girls (70%) are more likely to go to their parent(s) for information on career choices, compared to African American (54%) and Hispanic (54%) girls.

% WHO AGREE…	CAUCASIAN	AFRICAN AMERICAN	HISPANIC
I know someone in a STEM career.[2]	61	48	52
One or both of my parents are in a STEM career.[2]	29	18	23
I go to my parent(s) for information on career choices.[1]	70	54	54

[1] African American, Hispanic lower than Caucasian
[2] African American lower than Caucasian

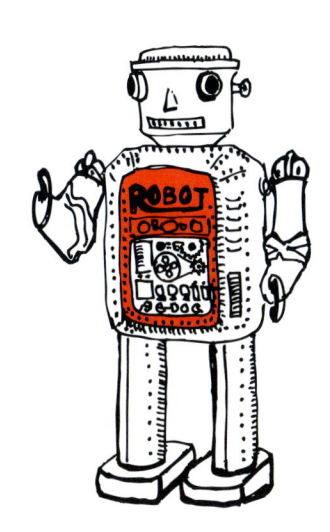

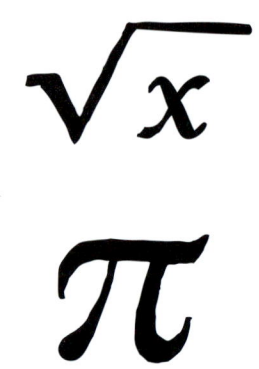

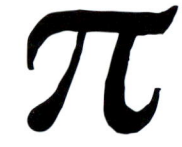

We found that adult support/encouragement appears to be lower for African American and Hispanic girls as well:

- African American girls (62%) say that teachers are less supportive of their career interests, compared to Caucasian girls (73%).
- African American girls (38%) say that their parents are less likely to approve of a STEM career compared to Caucasian girls (54%).

% WHO AGREE…	CAUCASIAN	AFRICAN AMERICAN	HISPANIC
Teachers are supportive of my career interests[1]	73	**62**	66
My mom is supportive of my career interests[3]	92	**86**	89
My dad is supportive of my career interests[1]	87	**75**	84
Friends are supportive of my career interests[2]	83	77	**73**
My mom encourages my questions and creativity about the world[2]	79	76	**69**

[1] African American lower than Caucasian
[2] Hispanic lower than Caucasian
[3] African American lower than Caucasian, 90% significance

Financial Motivations

Additionally, some new findings emerged. African American and Hispanic girls appear to value financial motivations in determining their career paths. For example:

- African American (41%) and Hispanic girls (31%) are more likely to be motivated to choose a career that pays a lot of money compared to Caucasian girls (21%).
- More Hispanic girls (67%) are likely to say that their mothers want them to choose a career that pays a lot of money compared to Caucasian girls (55%).

African American (21%) and Hispanic girls (21%) are less interested in being stay-at-home moms compared to Caucasian girls (38%).

% WHO AGREE…	CAUCASIAN	AFRICAN AMERICAN	HISPANIC
I'd rather choose a career that pays a lot of money (vs. a career that I really enjoy).[1]	21	**41**	**31**
My mother wants me to choose a career that pays a lot of money.[2]	55	59	**67**
My mother pressures me to pursue career plans that don't interest me.[2]	16	20	**26**

[1] African American, Hispanic higher than Caucasian
[2] Hispanic higher than Caucasian

Barriers and Obstacles

African American and Hispanic girls are more cognizant of gender barriers in STEM fields.

- Compared to Caucasian girls (19%), more African American (30%) and Hispanic girls (28%) worry about sexual harassment in the STEM workplace.
- More African American (35%) girls feel that employers in the fields of STEM don't usually want to hire women, compared to Caucasian girls (25%).
- Half (50%) of African American girls (compared to 38% of Caucasian girls) agree with the statement: "Because I am female, I would NOT be treated equally by the men I studied/worked with if I pursued a career in STEM."

% WHO AGREE…	CAUCASIAN	AFRICAN AMERICAN	HISPANIC
Because I am female, I would NOT be treated equally by the men I studied/worked with if I pursued a career in STEM.[1]	38	**50**	41
Employers in the fields of STEM don't usually want to hire women.[1]	25	**35**	31
Because I am female, I would be treated like an outsider if I pursued a career in STEM.[1]	25	**38**	29
If I went into a career in STEM, I'd worry about sexual harassment in the work place.[2]	19	**30**	28

[1] African American higher than Caucasian
[2] African American higher than Hispanic, Caucasian

Barriers as Motivators, Not Obstacles

All girls think that obstacles make them stronger (African American–92%, Hispanic—91%, Caucasian—88%) and feel motivated to prove people wrong who questions their capabilities (African American—92%, Hispanic—91%, Caucasian—92%).

These findings suggest that African American and Hispanic girls have strong internal assets such as confidence and the ability and desire to overcome obstacles, which appear to complement and support their high levels of interest in STEM despite reported lower levels of adult support, exposure, and academic achievement.

Girls in focus groups were asked to talk about the life of an imaginary woman in a STEM career. African American and Hispanic girls in one setting discussed the role of obstacles in the life of this imaginary woman as well as in their own lives:

> *When people say no, [imaginary woman in STEM] works harder because she wants to get everything; that is her goal. She gets frustrated at work when the guys don't support her ideas, but it makes her work harder and she becomes stronger. You can do whatever you want if you work hard and persist—but you have to have the skills. You have to prove them wrong. Don't give up. If they keep saying yes to everything, it's not good. It's good to have a certain amount of resistance; good for someone to tell you 'no,' because that will happen in your life. You'll act spoiled if everyone always tells you 'yes.' Barriers will make you stronger and persist. She persists because she has knowledge and dedication. Tired of hearing 'no'—you will get told 'no' a lot in your life. Just keep going and don't give up.*
>
> —girl group, Orlando, Florida

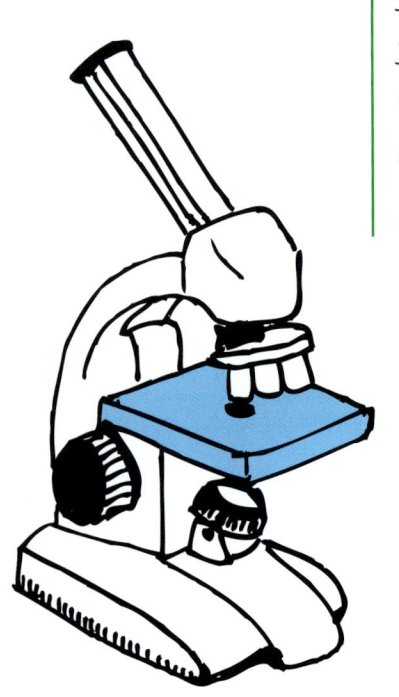

Summary and Discussion

There are two important take-aways from this research that have the potential to transform the national conversation about girls and young women in STEM:

1. As opposed to the past stereotype that even girls who perform well academically are not interested in STEM (because it is a "boy thing") our research demonstrates that interest among girls is there, it just needs to be primed.

2. The challenge that remains is how to turn girls' interest into action and make STEM the winner in the competition for girls' attention when it comes to career choices.

The following discussion explores what these mean in order to build girls' STEM futures.

Girls are Capable and Confident

Girls today have high aspirations and appear to be thinking differently about who they are and what they are capable of than those of past generations. We are encouraged by the number of girls who consider themselves hard workers and capable of doing whatever boys can do. Girls—regardless of STEM interest and racial/ethnic background—are confident and optimistic about their abilities and future endeavors. For example, nearly all (97%) girls say they will graduate from college, and a high percentage (84%) say they will go on to graduate school. While these rates are slightly inflated compared to actual data on higher education, it is encouraging, nonetheless, to know girls have such high aspirations for their futures. This is a great time for girls to think about possibilities and opportunities that may not have been presented to girls in the past or considered appropriate for girls. Past research[xvi] shows that low confidence and low perception of abilities hold girls back; we did not find that to be true for girls in our study. Girls are confident, say they are able to overcome obstacles, and don't see limitations getting in their way.

Girls Are Interested in STEM

We are very encouraged by the high level of interest girls have in STEM. Nearly three-quarters of girls we surveyed exhibit interest in STEM. This high rate is found across the three largest ethnic groups—Caucasian, African American, and Hispanic. To our knowledge, no research to date has shown findings this uplifting. Contrary to past research, our study shows that interest does not drop during middle school, but rather remains high, since nearly 74% of high school girls say they are interested. Some of the discrepancy between past studies and this study can be explained by the way STEM interest was measured. In past studies, girls' interest in STEM was measured more concretely, focusing on one area of STEM interest (e.g., computing) or on intentions to major in a STEM subject in college. Our measure of STEM dealt more with general interest in STEM fields, and measured STEM interest in the present, rather than in the future. Regardless, this high amount of interest suggests that this generation of girls may have different perceptions about STEM (perhaps also fueled by youth living more digitally than ever before) and shows that

> **The opportunity that exists for us is to support girls to have engaging experiences in the physical sciences. Often it is in the physical sciences where there is room for creativity, and for thinking outside the box.**
>
> Preeti Gupta, Ph.D., senior vice president for education and family programs, New York Hall of Science

> **Overall, it seems that the girls who are most interested in STEM take on challenges at many levels. They are challenging themselves in school, and challenging stereotypes and preconceived notions about what girls can and want to do. We need to ensure that more girls have the kinds of support, information, and encouragement needed for them to take on and overcome these challenges that limit their opportunities.**
>
> Andresse St. Rose, Ed.D, senior researcher, American Association of University Women (AAUW)

discussions about the lack of girls and women in STEM need to be reframed in a way that acknowledges that girls actually are interested. Future work and discussions should consider how girls can turn these interests into future STEM college majors and future STEM career involvement, so we don't "lose" these interested girls as they get older.

Our data show that girls interested in STEM tend to be interested in learning and asking questions about the world. This kind of interest—specifically, interest in knowing how things work, building things, putting things together, and designing technologies (i.e. video games/iPhone apps)—is high across racial/ethnic groups, and is in some cases higher for African American and Hispanic girls. Importantly, these are inherent characteristics of scientists, researchers, and engineers who ask big questions and determine the best ways to solve problems in their communities and for their country. They are also inherent characteristics of children, who like to explore the world around them and ask questions. Girls may identify more with the process of becoming an engineer than with the idea or label of being an engineer when they grow up. If girls are willing to learn and ask questions the same way STEM professionals ask questions and solve problems in the world, then girls are clearly capable of being successful in STEM fields and contributing in this line of work.

STEM Girls Stand Apart

Girls who are interested in STEM have something extra compared to girls who are not interested in STEM. In general, girls who are interested in STEM have been exposed to a variety of opportunities and support systems, and are high achievers. Compared to girls uninterested in STEM, they have higher academic achievement and interest in all school subjects, higher confidence in their STEM abilities, encouragement and exposure from adults, activity involvement in STEM subjects, and are more likely to know someone in a STEM career. African American and Hispanic girls are interested in STEM despite reported lower levels of STEM exposure, adult support, and academic achievement. For these girls, it appears that internal assets, such as confidence, a work ethic, high aspirations, and the ability/desire to overcome obstacles, help them to persevere and may possibly account for their high STEM interest. These findings show that it is important to foster girls' internal assets in addition to external factors, such as adult support and exposure to the possibilities that STEM fields can offer.

STEM Girls Have Many Options

STEM girls are interested in STEM careers as well as non-STEM careers, such as careers in entertainment, arts/design, and social science. They are well-rounded and have many options, supporting theories about choice for why girls and women are underrepresented in STEM fields.[xvi] On one hand, it's great that girls have well-rounded abilities and interests. On the other hand, STEM is consistently "losing" to other career options, such as teaching, and social services. The fact that more than 80% of girls are interested in a STEM career, but only 13% choose a STEM field as their top career choice shows that there is plenty of opportunity for bridging interest into distinct career plans for girls. The data show that a proportion of girls who say they are interested in STEM are leaning toward medical practitioner fields over other scientific careers that fall under traditional definitions of STEM, such as a medical scientist or a biotechnician, because of the perception of how these careers help people, which is a main draw for many girls.

Changing the World Through STEM

Girls want to change the world, and help people. Eighty-eight percent of all girls want to make a difference in the world, and 90% want to help people. Traditionally, they achieve this through careers working with people and are less likely to consider careers that use technology and scientific expertise to change the way things are done, to improve the environment, to make people healthier, or to make life more efficient. If more girls learn that STEM careers can still achieve their goals to help and serve, more girls will choose STEM.

African American and Hispanic girls have financial motivations in choosing a career path, fueled by their parents, and are less likely to say they want to be stay-at-home moms. It is important to note that some of these ethnic differences are confounded by and can be explained in part by socioeconomic status. Census data shows that low income families in the United States are more likely to be of African American and Hispanic descent.[xxv] Thus, these findings are likely to be related more to differences in socioeconomic status than ethnicity. STEM careers can fit well into any of these motivations, both financial and philanthropic.

There is plenty of opportunity for girls to be exposed to ways in which STEM careers can mesh with their motivations. By "marketing" STEM careers to girls the same way more common careers for women are promoted, we can ensure that more girls are intrigued by and choose STEM fields as their number one career choices. Unfortunately, STEM fields aren't as appreciated in the United States as they are in those countries that excel in STEM education and expertise. Entertainment culture appears to often clash with educational achievement for young people, especially girls, often making it "uncool" to be smart in subjects like math or science and a barrier to being noticed by boys.

> *I think sometimes girls don't want to go into STEM careers because women who do that are nerds and not the kinds of girls that guys are looking for sometimes.*
> —teen girl, Seattle, Washington

> **I was encouraged to see that helping people was the most important factor in choosing a career and that more STEM girls than non-STEM girls were 'most interested' in making a difference in the world. I think this is good news for the future direction of science and engineering.**
>
> Christianne Corbett,
> senior researcher,
> American Association of
> University Women (AAUW)

Limitations, But Opportunities for the Future

Gender barriers in STEM continue to exist and girls are aware of them. While the research shows that being aware of stereotypes can impact ability and performance—thus helping to confirm what the stereotype (such as "girls can't do math") says about a group[xii]—our research suggests that some girls do appear fueled by stereotype/gender barriers in STEM and want to challenge and overcome them. African American and Hispanic girls are particularly well aware of certain limitations and stigmas experienced by women in STEM careers, and this appears to motivate them to go against the odds and pursue these and other fields not typically expected for women or for individuals with their racial/ethnic background. Perhaps the girls who have strong internal assets (e.g., confidence) are more likely to challenge stereotypes; others might be less likely. However, few will want to continue to grapple with adversity for an extended period of time throughout their college lives and into their careers. Just as important as keeping teen girls highly interested in STEM fields is making certain that these fields are attractive enough for young women to remain and progress in throughout adulthood.

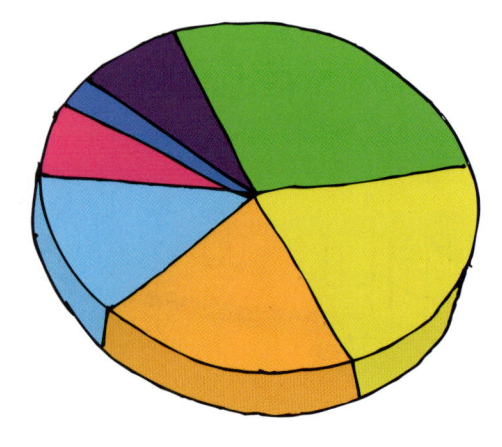

Implications and Recommendations for Future Work

Exposure and education—both formal and informal—will likely help send the message that STEM careers can help fulfill the desire to solve problems in the world and make the world a better place. Support and encouragement for STEM interest from adults, including parents, teachers, relatives, and mentors, goes a long way with girls. Paying attention to and fostering girls' internal assets, just as much as their formal education and training in important subjects like math and science, is critical. At a time when jobs are hard to find and higher education is necessary, it is more important than ever to show girls that STEM is the key to the future. As part of STEM advocacy efforts, Girl Scouts is promoting STEM solutions for girls at legislative hearings, briefings, community forums, and with the media in an effort to advance this important topic with community leaders and public officials at all levels.

The following is a list of recommendations for educators, parents, and supportive adults who work with and have relationships with girls.

1. Encourage young girls to ask questions about the world, to problem solve, and to use natural creativity through play, creativity, and experimentation. This inquisitiveness can lead to innovative work in the future. It is important to continue this growth in developmentally appropriate ways throughout childhood and adolescence—the phase where typically STEM interest has dropped.[xviii]

2. Foster girls' internal assets such as confidence, self-esteem, initiative, and a work ethic. This can make girls feel successful and capable when it comes to interest in STEM fields—and anything else they set their minds to and have traditionally been steered away from. When girls feel capable and confident in their abilities, they will be more likely to challenge themselves and obstacles along the way.

3. Expose girls to people who have careers in STEM, so they can observe firsthand what these careers are, and what they can offer. Girls can see the kinds of people who are in these careers, and begin to develop relationships with them. Girls can recognize how women in these fields have succeeded and overcome obstacles.

4. Keep girls interested and engaged in STEM over time and beyond transition points. While past research shows that girls' interest in STEM drops in middle school, this study points out another transition point—that girls' interest in STEM may be challenged by competing opportunities and interests as girls move from high school to college years and beyond. Providing college and career counseling for teen girls is important in bridging STEM interest in high school to a STEM major in college, eventually leading to a STEM career. Many high school girls say they are interested in STEM subjects and careers, but a much lower percentage say that a STEM career is their number one choice.

Most of the STEM girls enjoyed doing hands-on projects. Girl Scout STEM program activities provide girls with unique opportunities to experience hands-on science and engineering projects in a nonthreatening environment. The girls are more comfortable in exploring their interest in our programs since they are not being graded on their results and an all-girl environment also helps with increasing their comfort level. We hear often from our parents and troop leaders that these opportunities for hands-on STEM activities are becoming rare in traditional educational settings... We should continue to develop fun STEM activities for our girls.

Amy Hee Kim, Ph.D., manager, STEM program, Girl Scouts of Greater Los Angeles

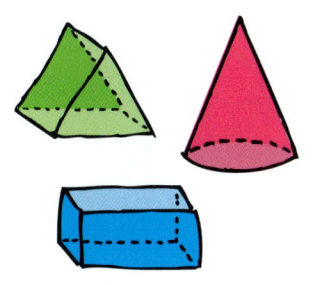

> I think highlighting how STEM fields can help people 'change the world' is critical. This aligns with other research done on engaging girls in science/engineering. It also provides a direct connection to the mission of Girl Scouting and the three keys to Leadership—Discover, Connect, and Take Action.
>
> Emily Fletcher, director of programs, Girl Scouts of Northeast Ohio

5. Support and encourage STEM interests. When supportive adults, such as parents, relatives, teachers, and mentors show an interest in STEM careers for girls, they make those fields seem much more realistic and feasible, rather than something untouchable or unreachable.

6. Show girls that what they want out of their careers can be achieved through STEM. Showing girls that they can change the world and help people through STEM, while also making a good salary, will help make STEM more of a priority for girls as they begin to think about and narrow down their college majors and career choices. Girls need more exposure to and understanding of what STEM careers entail to see that some of the ways of work they are already interested in—such as designing technologies, asking questions, and solving problems are the foundations of many STEM professions.

7. Many girls prefer working in groups and collaborating with others to solve problems. The perception is that the natural work culture of STEM professions tends to be isolating rather than inclusive. The work culture/environment (or the perception thereof) needs to be more people and team oriented for girls to find it appealing.

8. Steer clear of obvious or subtle stereotypes about girls' and women's abilities in math science. It is easy for girls to form attitudes about what girls and women should or should not be good at. Instead, model positive, more up-to-date words of encouragement that speaks to our generation of girls, that tell them they can be a STEM expert.

9. African American and Hispanic girls have just as much interest in STEM as Caucasian girls, yet they have had less exposure to STEM, lower academic achievement, and less adult support. Understanding these differences can help shape programming to the specific needs of targeted racial and ethnic populations of girls.

10. Use this research to create awareness and advocate for girls to be engaged in STEM opportunities. Become part of the conversation to get more girls involved and interested in STEM in order to improve their chances of engaging in a STEM career and to make STEM careers more accepting of women.

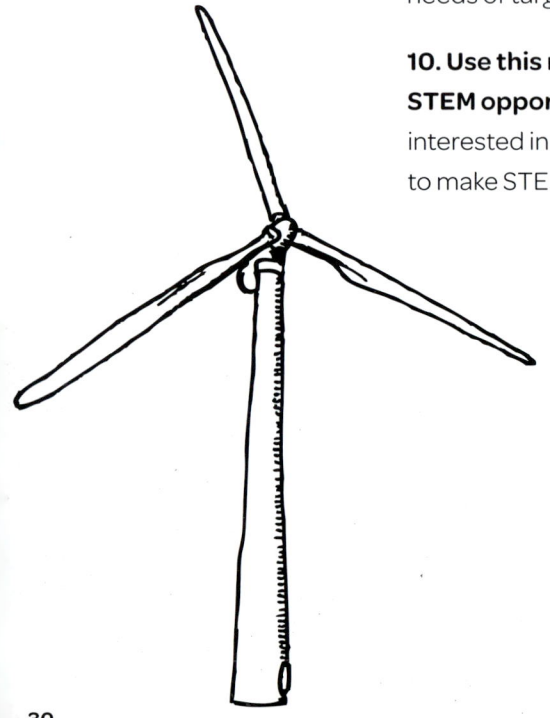

Appendix

Methodology

This project consists of original qualitative and quantitative research. The qualitative portion of the study consists of the results of several focus groups with girls to examine girls' perceptions and attitudes about STEM subjects and careers. Eleven focus groups of girls ages 8-18 were conducted in six diverse geographical locations in the United States—Austin, Texas; Seattle, Washington; Denver, Colorado; Orlando, Florida; Wilmington, Delaware; and Indianapolis, Indiana. The communities from which girls were recruited ranged from very large cities with populations over 2 million to smaller cities with populations of less than 100,000. These locations were chosen in collaboration with local Girl Scout councils, who helped provide groups of girls with STEM exposure as well as groups of girls without STEM exposure as a means of comparison. A total of 140 girls participated in focus groups, with an average of 12 participants per group. About half of the girls were Girl Scouts, and about half of the girls had some form of STEM exposure in the past (e.g., STEM camp, after-school program, Girl Scout event). Girls were a mix of racial/ethnic backgrounds; primarily Caucasian, African American, and Hispanic. This portion of the study was completed in March 2011.

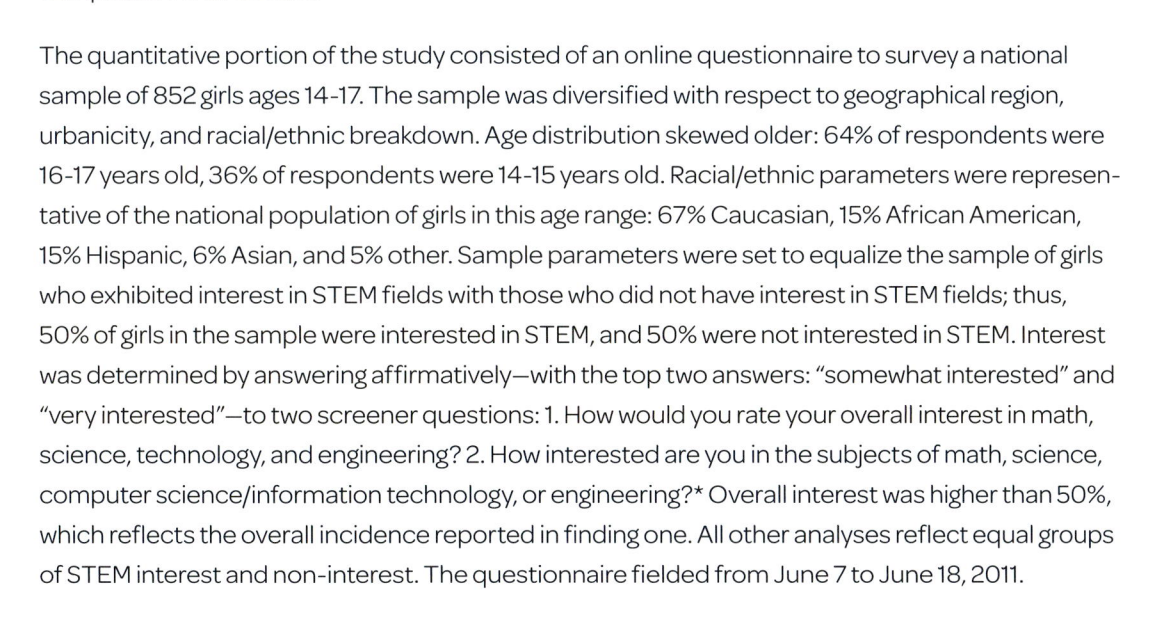

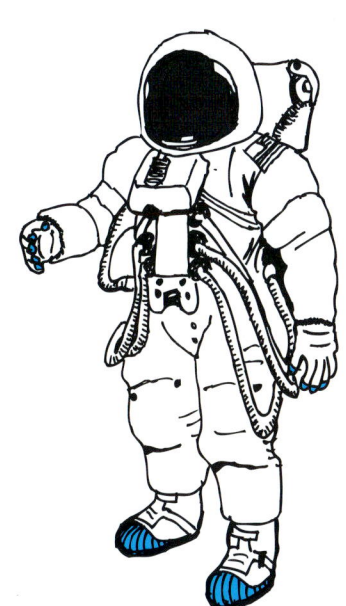

The quantitative portion of the study consisted of an online questionnaire to survey a national sample of 852 girls ages 14-17. The sample was diversified with respect to geographical region, urbanicity, and racial/ethnic breakdown. Age distribution skewed older: 64% of respondents were 16-17 years old, 36% of respondents were 14-15 years old. Racial/ethnic parameters were representative of the national population of girls in this age range: 67% Caucasian, 15% African American, 15% Hispanic, 6% Asian, and 5% other. Sample parameters were set to equalize the sample of girls who exhibited interest in STEM fields with those who did not have interest in STEM fields; thus, 50% of girls in the sample were interested in STEM, and 50% were not interested in STEM. Interest was determined by answering affirmatively—with the top two answers: "somewhat interested" and "very interested"—to two screener questions: 1. How would you rate your overall interest in math, science, technology, and engineering? 2. How interested are you in the subjects of math, science, computer science/information technology, or engineering?* Overall interest was higher than 50%, which reflects the overall incidence reported in finding one. All other analyses reflect equal groups of STEM interest and non-interest. The questionnaire fielded from June 7 to June 18, 2011.

*For question 2, respondents only needed to answer affirmatively to at least one subject.

References

[i] United States Department of Commerce. 2011. *STEM: Good jobs now and for the future.* Washington, DC: Economics and Statistics Administration.

[ii] United States Department of Education. 2008. *Highlights from TIMMS 2007: Mathematics and Science Achievement of U.S. Fourth- and Eighth-Grade Students in an International Context* (NCES 2009–001 Revised). Washington, DC: National Center for Education Statistics, Institute of Education Sciences.

[iii] Andreescu, T., J. A. Gallian, J. M. Kane, and J. E. Mertz. 2008. Cross-cultural analysis of students with exceptional talent in mathematical problem solving. *Notice of the American Mathematical Society*, 55(10): 1248-1260.

[iv] National Girls Collaborative Project. http://www.ngcproject.org/.

[v] GirlStart. www.girlstart.org.

[vi] United States Department of Education. 2010. Indicator 23. *The Condition of Education 2010*. Washington, DC: National Center for Education Statistics.

[vii] United States Department of Labor. 2009a. *Women in the labor force: A databook* (Report 1018). Washington, DC: Bureau of Labor Statistics.

[viii] National Science Foundation. 2008. S*cience and engineering degrees: 1966-2006* (Detailed Statistical Tables) (NSF 08-321). Arlington, VA: Division of Science Resources Statistics.

[ix] American Association of University Women. 2010. *Why so few? Women in science, technology, engineering, and mathematics*. Washington, DC: American Association of University Women.

[x] United States Department of Labor. 2009b. Bureau of Labor Statistics, *Employment and Earnings, 2009 Annual Averages* and *the Monthly Labor Review*.

[xi] Shettle, C. et al. 2007. *The Nation's Report Card: America's high school graduates: Results from the 2005 NAEP High School Transcript Study*. Washington, DC: United States Department of Education, Government Printing Office.

[xii] Walton, G.M. and S.J. Spencer. 2009. Latent ability: Grades and test scores systematically underestimate the intellectual ability of negatively stereotyped students. *Psychological Science*. 20(9): 1132-39.

[xiii] Nguyen, H. H. H. and A. M. M. Ryan. 2008. Does stereotype threat affect test performance of minorities and women? A meta-analysis of experimental evidence. *Journal of Applied Psychology* 93(6):1314-34.

[xiv] Aronson, J., C. B. Fried, and C. Good. 2002. Reducing the effects of stereotype threat on African American college students by shaping theories of intelligence. *Journal of Experimental Social Psychology* 38(2): 113-125.

[xv] Bisland, M., L. Kekelis, D. McCreedy, E. Koster, P. Gupta and C. Roman. 2011. Science Museum Roundtable. Discussion at the NCWIT K-12 Alliance summit, New York.

[xvi] Dweck, C. 2006. Is math a gift? Beliefs that put females at risk. In *Why Aren't More Women in Science? Top Researchers Debate the Evidence*, ed. S. J.Ceci and W. M. Williams, 47-55. Washington, DC: American Psychological Association.

[xvii] Halverson, H.G. 2011. The trouble with bright girls. *Huffington Post*, March 1. http://www.huffingtonpost.com/heidi-grant-halvorson-phd/girls-confidence_b_828418.html (accessed March 1, 2011).

[xviii] United States Department of Education. 2006. *The Condition of Education*. Washington, DC: National Center for Education Statistics, U.S. Government Printing Office.

[xix] Ceci, S.J., W. M. Williams, and S. M. Barnett. 2009. Women's underrepresentation in science: Sociocultural and biological considerations. *Psychological Bulletin* 135(2): 218-261.

[xx] Girl Scout Research Institute. 2008. *Change It Up! What Girls Say About Redefining Leadership*. New York: Girl Scouts of the USA.

[xxi] National Research Center for College and University Admissions. 2011. College major interest trends. Lee's Summit, Mo.: Report compiled for Girl Scouts of the USA.

[xxii] WGBH Education Foundation & Association for Computing Machinery. 2009. New image for computing: Report on market research.

[xxiii] Park, G., D. Lubinski and C. P. Benbow. 2008. Ability differences among people who have commensurate degrees matter for scientific creativity. *Psychological Science* 19: 957-961.

[xxiv] Fouad, N.A. and R. Singh. 2011. *Stemming the Tide: Why Women Leave Engineering*. Milwaukee: Center for the Study of the Workplace at the University of Wisconsin-Milwaukee. http://www.studyofwork.com/wp-content/uploads/2011/03/NSF_Women-Full-Report-0314.pdf.

[xxv] United States Census Bureau. 2010. Income, poverty, and health insurance coverage in the United States: 2009. *Current Population Reports*. Washington, DC: U.S. Government Printing Office.

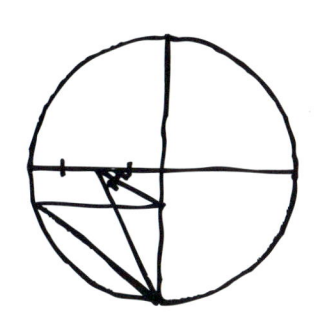

Resources

This list of organizations provides more information on STEM opportunities for girls.

Afterschool Alliance
Organization dedicated to raising awareness of the importance of afterschool programs and advocating for more afterschool investments; The Afterschool Alliance works to ensure that all children have access to affordable, quality afterschool programs.
www.afterschoolalliance.org

American Association for the Advancement of Science (AAAS)
International nonprofit organization dedicated to advancing science around the world.
www.aaas.org

American Association of University Women (AAUW)
Nationwide network of members, donors, branches, and college/university partners with the mission to advance equity for women and girls through advocacy, education, philanthropy, and research.
www.aauw.org

Association of Science-Technology Centers (ASTC)
Nonprofit organization of science centers and museums dedicated to furthering public engagement with science among increasingly diverse audiences; It encourages excellence and innovation in informal science learning by serving and linking its members worldwide and advancing their common goals.
www.astc.org

Biotechnology Institute
National educational organization with the mission to engage, excite, and educate as many people as possible, particularly young people, about biotechnology and its immense potential to heal the sick, feed the hungry, restore the environment, and fuel the economy.
www.biotechinstitute.org

Coalition for Science Afterschool
Strategic alliance of individuals and organizations from STEM education, youth development, and programs held outside of school time with the mission to coordinate and mobilize community stakeholders to strengthen and expand opportunities that engage young people in science after school.
www.afterschoolscience.org

CyberLearning Academy/National Education Foundation
Project that provides 21st century skills in math, science, technology, business, and test prep for disadvantaged students to close academic and digital gaps; The goal is to set up a Cyber-Learning Academy in most disadvantaged schools in the U.S. by 2020.
www.cyberlearning.org/k12education

Educate to Innovate
Federal campaign that includes efforts from leading companies, foundations, nonprofits, and science and engineering societies to work with young people across America to excel in science and math.
www.whitehouse.gov/issues/education/educate-innovate

FIRST
Nonprofit public charity with the mission to inspire young people to be science and technology leaders by engaging them in exciting mentor-based programs that build science, engineering, and technology skills, that inspire innovation, and that foster well-rounded life capabilities including self-confidence, communication, and leadership.
www.usfirst.org

Girl Scouts of the USA
Girl Scouts of the USA is the premiere leadership organization for girls, with the mission to build girls of courage, confidence, and character, who make the world a better place. Girls develop leadership and STEM skills through various national STEM program initiatives. One such initiative is *It's Your Planet—Love It!* Leadership Journey series which engages girls in kindergarten through the 12th grade in taking action to protect the planet. Another is the AT&T Imagine Series which piques high school girls' interest in STEM careers, while inspiring them through the Girl Scout Leadership Experience.
www.girlscouts.org

Girls, Math & Science Partnership
Partnership program of Carnegie Science Center with the mission to engage, educate, and embrace girls as architects of change, along with their parents, teachers, and mentors, in an effort to ensure that girls succeed in math and science.
www.braincake.org

Girls, Inc.
Nonprofit organization that inspires all girls to be strong, smart, and bold through research-based programs and advocacy that empower girls to reach their full potential and to understand, value, and assert their rights.
www.girlsinc.org

Great Minds in STEM
Nonprofit organization that aims to inspire and motivate underserved students to pursue careers in STEM.
www.greatmindsinstem.org

Great Science for Girls
Five-year initiative to broaden and sustain girls' interest and persistence in STEM, providing inquiry-based, informal science learning programs that will stimulate girls' curiosity, interest, and persistence in STEM and break down the barriers of gender stereotyping.
www.greatscienceforgirls.org

The Joan Ganz Cooney Center at Sesame Workshop
A Research center devoted to advancing children's learning through digital media through initiatives such as the STEM Challenge, which invites youth and adult game makers to show their passion for playing and making video games in order to motivate children's interests in STEM.
www.stemchallenge.org

Lockheed Martin
Global security and information technology company engaged in the research, design, development, manufacture, integration, and sustainment of advanced technology systems, products, and services.
www.lockheedmartin.com

NASA
Leading force in scientific research and in stimulating public interest in aerospace exploration, as well as science and technology in general.
www.nasa.gov

National Academy of Sciences (NAS)
Society of distinguished scholars engaged in scientific and engineering research who are dedicated to the use of science and technology for the general welfare.
www.nasonline.org

National Action Council for Minorities in Engineering
Organization that creates opportunities for underrepresented minority youth to receive educations in STEM disciplines and ensures successful graduates access to potentially exciting and rewarding careers.
www.nacme.org

National Alliance for Partnerships in Equity (NAPE)
Consortium of state and local agencies, corporations, and national organizations committed to the advancement of equity and diversity in classrooms and workplaces.
www.napequity.org

National Coalition of Girls' Schools (STEM page)
Global advocate for girls' education through collaboration with individuals, schools, and organizations dedicated to empowering girls to be influential contributors of the world.
www.ncrw.org

National Center for Women & Information Technology (NCWIT)
Coalition that works to increase diversity in IT and computing.
www.ncwit.org

National Girls Collaborative Project (NGCP)
Project designed to reach girl-serving STEM organizations across the U.S. that are committed to informing and encouraging girls to pursue careers in science, technology, engineering, and mathematics (STEM).
www.ngcproject.org

National Science Foundation (NSF)
Independent federal agency whose mission includes support for all fields of fundamental science and engineering, "to promote the progress of science; to advance the national health, prosperity, and welfare; to secure the national defense."
www.nsf.gov

National Science Teachers Association (NSTA)
Largest organization in the world committed to promoting excellence and innovation in science teaching and learning for all.
www.nsta.org

National Wildlife Federation
America's largest conservation organization to protect and restore wildlife habitat, confront global warming, and connect with nature.
www.nwf.org

Society of Women Engineers (SWE)
Nonprofit educational and service organization empowering women to succeed, advance, and be recognized for their life-changing contributions and achievements as engineers and leaders.
societyofwomenengineers.swe.org

The Center for Advancement of Informal Science Education (CAISE)
Partnership that works to strengthen and connect the informal science education community by catalyzing conversation and collaboration across the entire field, including youth, community, and after-school programs.
www.caise.insci.org

Techbridge Girls
Program to promote girls' interest and skills in science, technology, and engineering, through multi-faceted programs, as well as to develop resources for teachers, role models, families, and partners.
www.techbridgegirls.org

U.S. Department of Commerce

Federal department that promotes job creation, economic growth, sustainable development, and improved standards of living for all Americans by working in partnership with businesses, universities, communities, and our nation's workers.

www.commerce.gov

White House Council for Women & Girls

Coordinated Federal response to issues that particularly impact the lives of women and girls to ensure that federal programs and policies address and take into account the distinctive concerns of women and girls, including women of color and those with disabilities.

www.whitehouse.gov/administration/eop/cwg

Women's Bureau – US Department of Labor

Division of the Department of Labor which develops policies and standards and conducts inquiries to safeguard the interests of working women; to advocate for their equality and economic security for themselves and their families; and to promote quality work environments.

www.dol.gov/wb

Women in Engineering Pro Active Network (WEPAN)

National nonprofit organization which works to transform culture in engineering education to attract, retain, and graduate women with a clear focus on research-based issues and solutions.

www.wepan.org

YWCA

Oldest and largest multicultural women's organization in the world with the mission to eliminate racism and empower women.

www.ywca.org